Wow! Look What **Birds** Can Do!

KINGFISHER
LONDON & NEW YORK

Copyright © Macmillan Publishers International Ltd. 2020
Published in the United States by Kingfisher,
120 Broadway, New York, NY 10271
Kingfisher is an imprint of Macmillan Children's Books, London
All right reserved.

Distributed in the U.S. and Canada by Macmillan,
120 Broadway, New York, NY 10271
Library of Congress Cataloging-in-Publication data has been applied for.

Author: Camilla de la Bédoyère
Design and styling: Liz Adcock
Jacket design: Liz Adcock
Illustrations: Ste Johnson

ISBN 978-0-7534-7566-9 (hardback)
978-0-7534-7567-6 (paperback)

Copyright © Macmillan Publishers International Ltd. 2020

Kingfisher books are available for special promotions and premiums.
For details contact: Special Markets Department, Macmillan,
120 Broadway, New York, NY 10271.

For more information, please visit
www.kingfisherbooks.com

Printed in China
1 3 5 7 9 8 6 4 2
1TR/1019/WKT/UG/140WFO

Wow!
Look What
Birds
Can Do!

KINGFISHER
LONDON & NEW YORK

What is a bird?

**Watch out—there are lots of birds about!
More than 10,000 species in fact.**

All our feathered friends have beaks
and they lay eggs. The largest birds
are huge, but teeny-tiny ones are
smaller than your thumb!

I'm a runner, not a flyer!

Did you know?

A bird's feathers help
keep it warm, but they
can also help the
bird fly.

The largest bird is an ostrich.
It's as heavy as 75,000
bee hummingbirds!

I'm as big as an ostrich's eye!

Six million years ago there were monster birds in the sky. Argentavis was the size of a small plane.

I'm the **Largest** flying bird ever to exist!

My wings are verrrry Long!

I'm the **TALLEST** bird!

The tallest bird ever was the giant moa. It was too heavy to fly, but it could reach up into trees to nibble leaves. The moa birds became extinct 600 years ago.

A wandering albatross needs huge wings for flying far over the ocean. Its wingspan is 10 feet (3 meters) wide.

Wow!

Birds were alive at the same time as dinosaurs. The first birds lived 150 million years ago.

5

Beaks and feet

Birds have beaks, but no teeth. Beaks come in many shapes and sizes.

I reach into a flower to sip sugary nectar.

A sword-billed hummingbird has a super-long beak— it's longer than its body!

Wow!

A bird's beak is the perfect shape for the food it eats. Beaks are made of the same hard material that is in finger nails and rhino horns.

More fish please!

A pelican's huge beak scoops up water and fish. Its throat is made of stretchy skin, so it fills up like a bag!

My feet are made for swimming!

Birds can use their skinny legs and clawed toes for running, perching, walking, grabbing, and holding. Some birds, such as ducks, geese, albatrosses, and penguins, have webbed feet.

Did you know?

Birds with webbed feet are great swimmers. Their feet help push the bird through the water.

I put my foot in my mouth again!

A parrot can use its feet like hands to pick fruit and pop it in its mouth.

snip, snap, slurp!

A curlew's long, curved beak is great for slurping up worms, but a finch's small, strong beak is just right for cracking seeds open.

crack!

High flyers

Look up to the sky and watch us fly!
See us swoop, soar, glide, and dive.

Wow!

Only three types of animals can fly: birds, bats, and insects.

zooommm!

The fastest bird is the peregrine falcon. It dives through the air at 125 miles (200 kilometers) an hour, chasing other birds to eat!

catch me if you can!

Watch out birdie, here I come!

Most birds only fly forward, but hummingbirds can go forward, backward, sideways, and hover in one spot! They can spin, twist, and even fly upside down.

Many birds travel far to find food or a good place to lay eggs. Every year, Arctic terns fly from the Arctic to the Antarctic—they can fly 31,000 miles (50,000 kilometers) in just one year!

No wonder we're tired, we've flown the same distance as three trips to the Moon!

coming through . . . . . . Goose landing!

Did you know?

Birds need two feathery wings and huge muscles in their chests to fly. They also have holes in their bones, like a sponge, which help make their skeletons light.

Ducks and geese waddle on the ground, but they are superb swimmers and flyers. When they fly, they can reach speeds of more than 40 miles (64 kilometers) an hour!

Quick! Duck!

Eggs and nests

It's time to build a nest and lay eggs. Soon there will be hungry baby birds to feed.

A nest is usually made from twigs, leaves, and moss, but some birds use whatever they can find. Small birds often use sticky spiders' webs as glue. Lining a nest with feathers makes it soft and cosy.

oops! I've used too many feathers!

Hi friends!

Most birds nest away from other birds, but sociable weavers like company. Up to 500 birds work together to build giant nests from grass. Some of these nests have been used by birds for 100 years!

Some cave swiftlets make their nests using their spit—and nothing else! It dries hard, like powdered sugar. Some people think bird spit tastes nice and make soup with the nests!

My nest is good enough to eat!

A gray partridge lays up to 19 eggs at a time. That will be a lot of mouths to feed!

Hurry up, family, I want to play!

Up on the roof!

Wow!

A strange stork's nest was once found on top of a tower. It was made with hats, shoes, clothes, and even buttons!

Let me out!

11

Baby birds

Peek inside the nest to see
a clutch of cheeping chicks!

Male emus are wonderful
dads. They sit on the eggs
for about eight weeks, not
even leaving to eat. When
the chicks hatch, the dad
stays with them for a year.

You're the best, dad!

crack!

Dinner is served!

Wow!

Many chicks are bald,
blind, and completely
helpless when they hatch.
They need their parents to
keep them warm and feed
them for several weeks.

Wow!

An eggs contains everything that a chick needs to grow inside. Once the chick hatches, its parents are kept busy bringing food to the hungry baby.

Keep away or else mom will spit on you!

Like most birds, a fulmar takes good care of its chicks. It defends its nests by spitting out a nasty, smelly oil at any attacker that gets too close.

I think there's been a mix-up?

A cuckoo will lay an egg in another bird's nest. When the cuckoo chick hatches, it throws the other chicks and eggs out of the nest so it gets all the food!

Chatty birds

Birds are famous for their lovely songs, but they make other noises too!

I'm the greatest mimic!

Many birds can copy (or mimic) the sounds they hear, but marsh warblers are the best of all. They can learn the songs of more than 80 different species of birds!

my name is **Alex!**

Alex the gray parrot could say 150 words and even used them to tell people the color and shape of toys.

Ring-ring!

Starlings can mimic the sound of a phone's ringing!

Buzz! Snap! Pop!

Manakins sing with their wings. They rub their feathers to make "buzz," "snap," and "pop" noises!

Moooo! Mooooo!

The deep booming call of a bittern can be heard 3 miles (5 kilometers) away, and sounds like a mooing cow. A bellbird's song sounds like a tinkling bell!

Wow!

Male birds sing to find a partner, but most birds can make a loud alarm call to warn if there is danger nearby.

Tinkle! Tinkle!

15

Show-offs

Male birds love to put on a good show. They dress to impress and dance to display their fine feathers.

A bowerbird doesn't just dance—he makes his own dance floor and decorates it! He builds a leafy shelter with grass and adds anything colorful he can find, including beads, ribbons, and toys!

I look good on the dance floor.

Hey, it's party time!

When a male frigatebird spies a female, he turns on the charm. He spreads his wings, throws back his head, and fills his red throat with air. It looks like a big red balloon!

Did you know?

Good looks really matter to birds so it's no wonder that they have great eyesight. Birds can see in color and pick out three times more detail than a human can.

I've got my eyes on you!

Oi...

A male peacock has long tail feathers that are glossy green and blue, and marked with eye-spots. To impress a female peacock (a peahen), he spreads out his tail like a fan and shakes, so the feathers shimmer in the light.

Hungry birds

Worms are juicy and seeds are tasty, but birds eat lots of other things too.

Skuas are called pirates of the sky because they dive-bomb other birds and steal their fish!

Yo-ho-ho!

slurp!

Get off my fish!

Shrikes have disgusting table manners. They catch bugs and stick them on sharp twigs or barbed wire so they can eat them more easily. The bugs wriggle, but they can't escape.

Stop wiggling, you're bugging me!

18

Grrr . . . I'm called **the tiger of the sky.**

HeLp!

A sparrowhawk has a big appetite, gobbling around 8,000 smaller birds a year.

Did you know?

More than 1,500 species of birds eat flowers. They feed on the sweet nectar and pollen that grow inside.

A toucan's huge beak is useful for reaching the fruits at the far end of a spindly branch.

Mmmmm, blood!

Wow!

Song thrushes use rocks to smash snails so they can get to the juicy body inside.

Smash!

The vampire ground-finch will stand on a boobie's back and peck holes in the bigger bird's skin. Then it drinks the blood that oozes out. Strangely, the boobie doesn't seem to mind!

who's this?

Walkabout

Why fly when you can walk or run everywhere? These birds prefer to stay close to the ground.

I'm a cassowary.

careful, I'm deadly!

The cassowary's sharp claws grow up to 4 inches (10 centimeters) long! This fast runner kicks anything in its way, slashing with its knifelike toes. It also swims and can leap 7 feet (2 meters) into the air.

Wow!

Ostriches, rheas, emus, and cassowaries are big birds that can't fly. Their great size, super-speedy running skills, and strong kicks keep them safe. Called ratites, these birds are so fast they can race cars!

I'm a speedy roadrunner.

Roadrunners can fly, but they prefer to snatch insects while running. Reaching speeds of 26 miles (32 kilometers) an hour, roadrunners are such nifty movers they can catch and kill rattlesnakes!

Wow!

Flightless birds still have wings, but they are too small for flying. Their feathers are often soft and fluffy to keep the bird warm instead.

I wish I'd taken **flying lessons** after all . . .

The dodo was a large flightless bird that built its nest on the ground. It became extinct after humans moved onto its island home and brought cats, dogs, and rats that ate its chicks and eggs.

Perfect penguins

Black bodies fly through the water, speeding after fish. Watch out—the penguins are coming!

Emperor penguins can dive deep in the ocean, where it's dark and cold. They hunt fish and squid and can hold their breath for more than 10 minutes at a time!

Huddle!!!

Did you know?

Penguins' wings work like flippers for flying through water instead of air. Their chubby bodies are packed with fat to keep them warm.

Galapagos penguins live farther north than other penguins, where it's warmer. They rest their flippers on their feet so they don't get sunburned!

Let's dive down deep!

Wow!

Penguins often give their mates a pebble as a special present to say "I love you!"

The gentoo is the fastest underwater bird, but it also surfs! These penguins love playing in the waves so much that they swim to find the best ones to surf, then swim back out to have another go!

We love to surf!

Love you!

Thanks, dad!

Male emperor penguins have a big flap of tummy skin that works like a snuggly body blanket. They lay it over their chicks, who sit on their feet. It keeps them safe and warm.

You'll get sunburn . . .

Rockhoppers have snazzy yellow head feathers called a crest. They are super-bouncy and like to leap out of the water onto rocks, dive into waves, and jump over ice.

Wheeeee!

Water birds

Water birds live near rivers, ponds, and lakes where they can always find plenty of food.

Let's go swimming!

As soon as ducklings can walk they follow their mother to water and can swim right away. If they see another animal before they see their mother, they start to follow them instead!

Just chilling.

This floating nest belongs to a great crested grebe. Keeping chicks on an island is a smart way to keep them safe!

over here crocs!

This odd bird is called a shoebill because its beak—or bill—is shaped like a shoe. It stands in the water watching, then pounces on anything that moves. It even attacks crocodiles and turtles!

Wow!

Waterbirds also use their beaks to clean their feathers and spread natural body oil over them, so they are sleek, smooth, and waterproof.

Flamingos can eat only when their heads are upside down! They are pink because they eat pink food that they find in water.

Think pink!

Many waterbirds have long spear-shaped beaks that they use to stab fish. Spoonbills have beaks that are big and broad, like a spoon. They sweep their mouth from side to side, scooping up insects and fish.

My bill can sense small animals— there's no escape!

I can touch the bottom of the river!

Did you know?

Wading birds don't need rubbers. They have long legs so they can walk into the water and feed. Stilts have the longest legs for their body size.

Birds of prey

Beware of these birds. They have huge, hooked beaks and sharp claws for grabbing and stabbing!

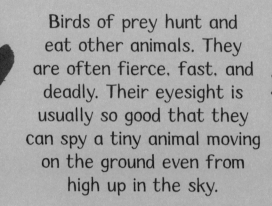

Birds of prey hunt and eat other animals. They are often fierce, fast, and deadly. Their eyesight is usually so good that they can spy a tiny animal moving on the ground even from high up in the sky.

My sharp claws are called **talons**.

Wow!

The largest bald eagle nest recorded is 3 tons—the same weight as a small Asian elephant.

Full stomach and still clean!

Vultures eat dead animals. They have bald heads so it's easier to keep their faces clean after they've eaten a rotting, stinky meal!

The soft, downy feathers on an owl's legs and wings help muffle the sound of it flying—so they can swoop silently on their prey.

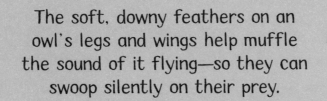

Fluffy feet!

Going higher!

Squawk!

The largest birds of prey are Andean condors. They soar above mountains on warm winds that lift them up high. A condor's wingspan can measure 10 feet (3 meters) from wingtip to wingtip!

Wow!
Great horned owls snack on whole rats and mice, but they also attack dogs and even young alligators!

Pass the sick bucket!

Owls often swallow their food whole. They vomit up the hard body bits that they can't digest, such as bones and teeth. You can open up one of these pellets to see what an owl has been eating!

Birds and people

We love birds! We can help them by cleaning up litter and providing a water bath.

Please let me out!

Many parrots, like this Spix's macaw, are struggling to survive because their rainforest home has been cut down and people catch them to sell as pets.

People call us clowns of the sea, but we're not laughing now.

Puffins are brightly colored seabirds that catch sand eels to feed their chicks. Humans have been catching so many sand eels that now the puffins don't have enough left for their families.

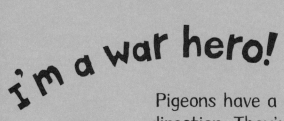

I'm a war hero!

Pigeons have a great sense of direction. They've been used to carry messages and 32 pigeons have been awarded a medal for their great courage in wartime. GI Joe was a pigeon that took messages that helped save the lives of at least 100 soldiers.

Did you know?

Sadly, people have not looked after birds or their homes. Some birds are very close to going extinct, including the giant ibis. There are fewer than 200 of these birds alive in the whole world.

We're in DANGER!

People keep chickens so they can eat their eggs. Sometimes, laying hens lose their feathers so people knit snug sweaters to keep them warm.

Is this a worm?

Strange but true

Welcome to the bizarre world of birds, where weird things happen!

I'm poisonous!

The skin and feathers of a hooded pitohui contain poison. These birds get the poison from eating beetles and it helps keep them safe from attack.

You scratch your back . . .

. . .and I'll scratch mine!

Penguins have such loose neck joints they can scratch their own backs with their beaks. From the front they look headless!

Bad luck! I'm a snake killer!

Secretary birds can kill deadly snakes. They either stamp on them or they carry them into the air and drop them from a great height. That's a couple of ways to avoid getting a nasty bite!

Birds often fly in big groups called flocks. The red-billed quelea can gather in flocks of millions. Each bird weighs only as much as a few grapes, but when many birds settle on a tree, the weight can break branches!

I'm not sure we can get any more on here . . .

Did you know?

Birds can't sweat so if they get too hot, they might die.

If you were up to your knees in smelly bird poop, would you be smiling? You might if you knew that guano (that's the proper name for bird poop) is used to make plants grow. Farmers love it and it's worth a lot of money!

Our poop is very useful!

Night, night birds

The sun is going down, but these busy birds are getting up!

Whiskered auklets nest in dark caves. They have whiskers, like a cat, to feel their way in the darkness. The whiskers are made of short, stiff feathers.

Wow!

Animals that are active at night are called nocturnal. Finding food in the dark can be hard, so nocturnal animals often have a good sense of smell or amazing eyesight.

I am not a cat!

My eggs are precious.

One of the strangest, and rarest, birds is a flightless parrot called a kakapo. Today, there are only about 150 of these precious birds alive. They are protected on an island where scientists take care of them.

BOO!

Owls have huge, round eyes and amazing eyesight—their night vision is 100 times better than ours.

I'm so fluffy!

Kiwis spend the day in a burrow, but come out at night to hunt for earthworms. Kiwis cannot fly and their feathers look like fluffy fur.